i did it without thinking

QUICK DECISIONS CAN HAVE LONG-TERM CONSEQUENCES. THAT'S WHY YOU WANT TO MAKE SMART DECISIONS ABOUT DRUGS AND ALCOHOL, SCHOOL, FRIENDS, AND YOUR BODIES. TAKE THIS QUIZ TO TEST HOW MUCH YOU KNOW ABOUT THE LONG-TERM CONSEQUENCES OF REAL-LIFE CHOICES.

True or False?

1 Fewer than a quarter of teen males who father a child marry the mother of that child.

2 Being sent to juvenile detention isn't anything like going to prison.

3 Most teens who drop out of school end up going back or earning an equivalency degree called a GED.

4 Talking about someone behind his or her back is a harmless activity that never leads to trouble.

5 The risks of losing a lot of money while gambling on the Internet are low.

6 Most states prohibit anyone younger than 18 from getting a tattoo or body piercing.

7 Most teens who decide not to drink alcohol or take drugs end up having boring social lives.

8 There are many opportunities for teens to volunteer to help those in need.

Answer key:
(1) True; **(2)** False; **(3)** False; **(4)** False;
(5) False; **(6)** True; **(7)** False; **(8)** True

Chapter one: The material on pages 8–15 was originally published in "The Brain Game," by Denise Rinaldo, *Scholastic Choices*, February/March 2006; **Chapter two: Nick's story** was originally published in "On the Lockdown," by Karen Fanning, *Scholastic Choices*, March 2002. **John's story** was originally published in "High Stakes," by Karen Fanning, *Scholastic Choices*, October 2006. The information in the sidebar on page 24 is from the Office of Juvenile Justice and Delinquency Prevention Statistical Briefing Book; **Chapter three: Nancy's story** was originally published in "Mama Drama," by Alexandra Rockey Fleming, *Scholastic Choices*, January 2005. **Aggie's story** was originally published in "Joy and Pain," by Karen Fanning, *Scholastic Choices*, January 2006. **Akeem's story** was originally published in "Father's Day, EVERY DAY," by John DiConsiglio, *Scholastic Choices*, January 2007. The information on page 36 is from www.surebaby.com; **Chapter four:** Doreen's story was originally published in "Tale of a Dropout," by John DiConsiglio, *Scholastic Choices*, October 2004. The information on page 53 is from the U.S. Census Bureau 2006 American Community Survey; **Chapter five: Anne's story** was originally published in "Out of Control," by Leah Paulos, *Scholastic Choices*, November/December 2006; **Chapter six: Fawna's and Heidi's stories** were originally published in "Bodily Harm," by John DiConsiglio, *Scholastic Choices*, January 2005; **Chapter seven: Mack's story** was originally published in "Lifesaver!" by John DiConsiglio, *Scholastic Choices*, January 2006. **Candi's story** was originally published as "Rescue Hero," by Laura Linn, *Scholastic Choices*, November/December 2005; **Chapter eight: Caitlin's and Colleen's stories** were originally published in "Drug-Free and Proud," by Leah Paulos, *Scholastic Choices*, October 2006. The information in the sidebars on pages 87 and 88 is from the National Center on Addiction and Substance Abuse at Columbia University; **Chapter nine: Amelia's story** was originally published as "Helping the Homeless," by Karen Fanning, *Scholastic Choices*, October 2005.

Photographs © 2008: Alamy Images: 44, 46 (Bubbles Photolibrary), 38 (Jacky Chapman/Janine Wiedel Photolibrary), 69 (Olaf Doering), 5, 101 (Ian Shaw), 99 (Paul Wood), 35 (David Young-Wolff); AP Images: 18 (Chet Brokaw), 22 (Rob Carr); Beth Dixson Photography: 68; Corbis Images: 13 (Heide Benser/zefa), 30 (Peter Dench), 11 (Randy Faris), 54 (Jon Feingersh/zefa), 52 (Peter M. Fisher), 92 (Carlos Avila Gonalez/San Francisco Chronicle), 73 (Ilona Habben/zefa), 16, 23 (Norbert Huettermann/zefa), 9 (Will & Deni McIntyre), 51 (moodboard), 81 (Richard T. Nowitz), 94 (Reuters), 6 (Zave Smith), 55 (Michel Touraine/pixland), 8 (Visuals Unlimited); Getty Images: 56, 74, 78 (Absodels), 4, 15 bottom (Paul Costello), 50 (Andy Crawford), 14 top (Joanne Dugan), 64 (Nabil John Elderkin), 63 (Blasius Erlinger), 66 (Hola Images), 41 (Christina Kennedy), 43 (Richard Koek), 76 (Kieran Scott), 25 (Siri Stafford), cover (Dougal Waters), 21 (Erik Von Weber), 86 (Caroline Woodham); JupiterImages/Mike Kemp: 82, 85; Photo Researchers, NY/John Bavosi: 10; PhotoEdit: 33 (Bill Aron), 27 (Colin Young-Wolff); Superstock, Inc.: 32 (BananaStock), 60, 61 (Brand X); The Image Works/Bob Daemmrich: 97; VEER: 15 top, 59 (Fancy Photography), 14 bottom (Andrea London/Solus Photography).

The photos in this book are for illustration purposes only and do not depict the real people profiled in this book.

Cover design: Marie O'Neill
Book production: The Design Lab
CHOICES editor: Bob Hugel

Library of Congress Cataloging-in-Publication Data
Hugel, Bob, 1964–
 I did it without thinking : true stories about impulsive decisions
that changed lives / by Bob Hugel.
  p. cm.
 Includes bibliographical references and index.
 ISBN-13: 978-0-531-13868-7 (lib. bdg.)   978-0-531-20526-6 (pbk.)
 ISBN-10: 0-531-13868-2 (lib. bdg.)   0-531-20526-6 (pbk.)
 1. Adolescent psychology—Juvenile literature. 2. Risk-taking
(Psychology) in adolescence—Juvenile literature. 3. Decision making in
adolescence—Juvenile literature. I. Title.
 BF724.H79 2008
 155.5'18—dc22   2008000690

SCHOLASTIC CHOICES

True stories
about impulsive
decisions that
changed lives

i did it without thinking

Bob Hugel

Franklin Watts®

AN IMPRINT OF SCHOLASTIC INC.
NEW YORK • TORONTO • LONDON • AUCKLAND • SYDNEY
MEXICO CITY • NEW DELHI • HONG KONG
DANBURY, CONNECTICUT

wired
to act

A LOOK INSIDE THE TEEN BRAIN

In this book, you'll read about lots of teens who made impulsive decisions that affected the rest of their lives. Some of these decisions were heroic. Others were regrettable. And some were disastrous.

But before you dive into these stories, have a look inside the teen brain. Is it wired to consider options wisely—or to act impulsively?

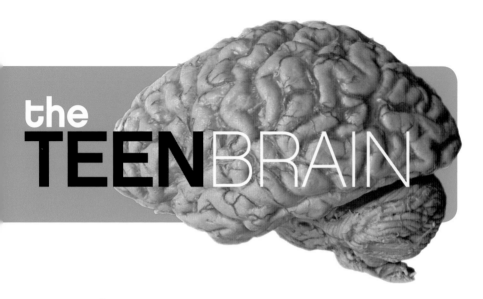

the
TEENBRAIN

The Teen Brain

Why do teens act impulsively? What prevents a teen from thinking about the consequences of breaking the law, having unprotected sex, or trying drugs? A teen's family environment plays a role in the decisions he or she makes. The kinds of friends a person has also influences what he or she does. But there's something else that plays a major role in why teens behave the way they do: their brains.

Dr. Jay Giedd of the National Institute of Mental Health in Bethesda, Maryland, is a world-renowned brain researcher. Since 1991, he has been studying the brains of kids using a technique called **magnetic resonance imaging (MRI)**, which allows researchers to see how brains respond to events and experiences. He has tracked these kids from early childhood through their teen years.

Giedd's findings have been groundbreaking. Before he began his work, scientists thought the brain stopped developing at around age 12. But Giedd's MRI studies revealed that right around puberty, the brain undergoes a huge brain-cell growth spurt. Right after that, the brain starts to prune itself by slashing back its number of brain cells. At the same time, connections between the brain cells that remain are strengthened and cemented.

"You're eliminating some connections and making remaining ones stronger," Giedd says. "You wind up with fewer, but faster connections." The brain-cell pathways you don't use are destroyed. Those you do use are strengthened. "It's use it or lose it," he says.

During this time, a teen's brain is shaped by experience. For example, if you spend a lot of time playing basketball and practicing the piano, those brain-cell connections will survive and grow stronger.

As Giedd and other brain researchers watched teens' brains develop, they discovered that some parts of the brain develop before others. As it turns out, the part of the brain that matures last is the **prefrontal cortex**. (Knock on the top of your forehead, just where your hair starts. That's your prefrontal cortex.) This is the part of your brain in charge of decision making and

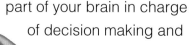

limbic system

prefrontal cortex

impulse control. The cells in this part of your brain are pruned back, and the remaining connections strengthen only after pruning has happened in all other parts of the brain.

What does this mean? While other areas of your brain are all trimmed and organized, your prefrontal cortex is still in a jumble.

As a result, it can be hard for teens to make well-considered decisions, especially when they have to decide quickly. When you're trying to make a snap decision—"Should I ride my bike down this stairway?" or "Should I run that yellow light?"—nerve impulses in your brain bounce all over the place.

A teen's brain is shaped by experience.

Giedd says the prefrontal cortex isn't fully developed in most people until about age 25. While your prefrontal cortex is still developing, your brain's emotional center—the **limbic system**—is responsible for your actions. Eventually, your prefrontal cortex will become the brakes for this "act first, think later" part of your brain—but that hasn't fully happened yet for teens.

Does this mean that teens aren't responsible for their decisions? Does this mean they're off the hook the next time they suddenly decide to look at another student's test answers in class or impulsively throw a punch at someone who's giving them a hard time? The answer is no. Your brain may be doing things that are beyond your control, but that doesn't mean that you have zero control over your brain.

The key is to learn to pause and give yourself time to think before you act. Research shows that when teens are given time to mull over their options, they make sound decisions about risk. The prefrontal cortex can override the limbic system. "The fact that your brain is still changing creates enormous abilities to learn and optimize to different environments," Giedd says. So just because you're wired to act impulsively doesn't mean you have to.

think it
THROUGH

Giedd recommends taking the following steps to avoid making rash decisions that could lead to trouble.

PAUSE and think about your options before acting. If you have time, write down a list of your options and look them over. And don't be afraid to ask others for advice, especially people who can look at the situation calmly.

TALK to adults you respect about how they make decisions. As annoying as adults can be to teens, many do have experience dealing with difficult decisions. Tap into that expertise.

ASK your parent or guardian to let you participate in family decisions. Watch how they weigh different factors. Keep their techniques in mind when you make decisions of your own.

acting
on impulse

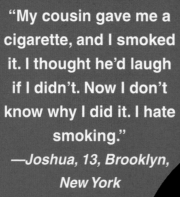

"My cousin gave me a cigarette, and I smoked it. I thought he'd laugh if I didn't. Now I don't know why I did it. I hate smoking."
—*Joshua, 13, Brooklyn, New York*

"A kid insulted the pants I was wearing. He said they were geeky or something. I pushed him as hard as I could against this cement wall. I couldn't believe I did that. Luckily, he was okay."
—*Thomas, 16, Albuquerque, New Mexico*

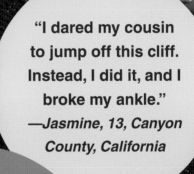

"I dared my cousin to jump off this cliff. Instead, I did it, and I broke my ankle."
—*Jasmine, 13, Canyon County, California*

"I left my house and went to my friend's house without telling anyone. My grandmother died, and no one could find me."
—*Araceli, 12, Canyon County, California*

behind bars

"I MEANT IT AS A JOKE"

Nick's Story

Having skipped class, Nick wanted to avoid getting caught, so he hid in the bathroom of his high school. "No one else was in there," he says. "I was bored so I lit the hole underneath the soap dispenser with a lighter to clog the soap. I meant it as a joke."

But it was no joke. When Nick tried to put out the flame with a paper towel, the towel caught on fire. "I tried to put it out with another paper towel, but that caught on fire too," he says.

Mistakenly thinking that the fire would put itself out, Nick left the bathroom. A fellow student walked into the restroom and was greeted by a big cloud of black smoke. The student pulled the fire alarm, the school was evacuated, and the fire department arrived. Soon a police detective was at the scene asking questions.

"People had seen me go in the bathroom earlier, so the detective approached me," Nick says. "I tried to deny what I had done. I told him some lies.

"Later that night, the police asked me to come down to the police station because my story was a little fishy. They asked me more questions. They didn't believe my story. I was charged with setting a fire. The police read me my rights—right in front of my parents."

The incident was not the first time Nick, who lives in Boston, Massachusetts, broke the law. When he was 14, he stole $800 from a teacher's purse.

After getting caught, he pleaded guilty to **larceny** and got six months of probation and had to do 20 hours of community service.

The legal system treated his second offense more harshly. Nick was sentenced to serve six months in a **juvenile detention facility**, a prison for teenagers. He had to share a small one-window room with two other inmates.

His days were strictly regimented. "Every morning, the guards woke us up at 8:30," he says. "They'd let us out to brush our teeth and comb our hair. Then we'd get locked back in our rooms until breakfast. We had to march to breakfast in a straight line. The guards would look straight down the line and if there was one head poking out, they wouldn't let us move. Wherever we went, we had to march in a line.

"The police read me my rights—right in front of my parents."

"Anywhere I went, I had to say, 'step in' and 'step out.' If I went to the bathroom, I had to say 'step in' and wait for a guard to say yes. Having my every move supervised made me feel powerless. I couldn't eat when I wanted. I couldn't go to bed when I wanted."

At meals, there was a three-person limit to each table. Inmates were forbidden to talk to inmates at other tables. "If the guard felt like we were eating too slowly, there would be no talking allowed at the table," Nick says. Inmates were allowed to shower, but got only three minutes to do so. By 9 P.M., every inmate was locked in his room, and lights were turned off an hour later.

Most of the daytime was spent in school, but Nick says the quality of the education was poor. "We had all the regular

> **"Having my EVERY MOVE supervised made me FEEL POWERLESS. I couldn't eat when I wanted. I couldn't go to bed when I wanted."**

classes like math, English, science, and social studies, but it was like being in second grade because the classes were so easy," he says.

The inmates were allowed to go outside for only an hour and a half each day. They'd play dodgeball, T-ball, football, and basketball. But the sight of the walls topped with barbed wire that surrounded the facility reduced any fun.

Breaking the rules or causing trouble was handled harshly. "You'd have to go to the time-out room," Nick says. "The guard put you in there until you calmed down. There was nothing in the room; it was like solitary confinement. You couldn't have contact with other residents. Sometimes, kids didn't come out of that room for days. If a kid had to stay there for several days, the guards would throw in a blanket and pillow."

Even having visitors provided little relief from the stress of being **incarcerated**. "Visits from my parents made me more depressed," Nick says. "It embarrassed me that my parents had to go through a metal detector to visit me. I wasn't spending any quality time with them. We always talked about my court case, and the staff was always staring at us to make sure I didn't do anything wrong. I was surrounded by my imprisonment and didn't feel comfortable talking to my parents at all."

Sadly, Nick's troubles didn't end with his release. Four months after getting out, he got busted for possessing marijuana. He was then placed in a juvenile rehabilitation program. He had to go to a juvenile detention facility for 70 days, and he had to attend daily group therapy sessions.

Upon his release, Nick's whereabouts had to be accounted for constantly. "A tracker called my house every night and made sure I was home by my curfew, which was 9 P.M.," Nick says. "Sometimes, the tracker showed up at my house unannounced. He also made sure I attended school. He called my teachers to make sure I was going to class. I had to report three times a week for group therapy. I didn't feel free at all, but it was better than being locked up. Now, I go to group therapy once a week, and my curfew has gotten later."

"I didn't feel free at all."

Nick says his time behind bars has made him grow up. He has not touched marijuana since being placed in the juvenile rehab program. "I've been taught a lesson," he says. "I'm going into my adult life knowing what imprisoned life is like. I appreciate the beautiful house I live in. I appreciate everyone who has tried to help me—my lawyers, my probation officer, and especially my family."

There are times when Nick looks back on his past deeds and shakes his head in dismay. "I'm an impulsive kid," he says. "I didn't think about anything before I did it. I wasn't thinking about how people would feel afterward—my family, the people I violated. I was just thinking about myself. It's especially hard on my parents. I want to tell kids, 'Think before you act.'"

15%

TEEN
ARRESTS

In 2005, 15 percent of all arrests involved persons under the age of 18.

John's Story

John never ended up in jail. But he also broke the law, and it got him in big trouble.

John fell victim to a gambling problem. At 14, he won $10 playing poker with friends. It wasn't much money, but the rush got him hooked. He was so intent on winning that he began cheating to win card games.

Then he took the next step by using his aunt's credit card to play poker online. "She had loaned me the card to use in emergencies, but I abused it big time," John says. "I racked up a $2,500 bill. I couldn't believe I lost that much money."

John's gambling isn't unique among his age group. Seventy percent of kids age 17 or younger in the United States have gambled in the past year, reports the National Council on Problem Gambling. And an estimated 2.9 million young people between the ages of 14 and 22 gamble on cards each week, according to the 2005 National Annenberg Risk Survey of Youth.

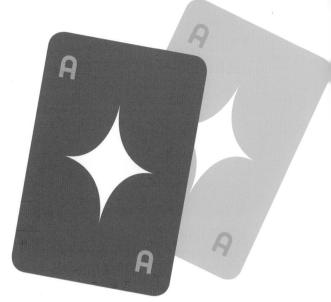

"GAMBLING is a game of CHANCE, and chances are you won't win."

John craved the excitement that came with playing cards. "It was an adrenaline rush," he says. "My heart would beat really fast. I would lose all control. I could not quit playing. I would play until I was out of money."

Losing is the norm when it comes to gambling. "Gambling is a game of chance, and chances are you won't win," says Dan Romer, director of the Adolescent Risk Communication Institute at the University of Pennsylvania. "For every person who is winning, there are a lot of other people who are losing."

John's desire to gamble led him to the Internet, where there are more than 2,500 gambling sites. Internet gambling is illegal in the United States.

However, the federal government cannot police online companies that operate outside the country. Gambling opponents contend that these businesses deliberately target underage gamblers.

Young people say they have little trouble getting around security devices that are supposed to stop them from gambling online. The first time John tried, it took just a few clicks of his mouse to get a seat at a virtual card table. "The site asked me if I was 18 and I said yes," says John, who was actually 15 at the time. "Then it asked me for a credit-card number and I entered it right off my aunt's card. I filled in the information in a matter of seconds and went straight into a poker game."

It didn't take long for John to start losing lots of money gambling online. That led to feelings of anxiety and depression. He quit playing football and lost interest in his schoolwork, barely managing to keep a D average.

John finally came to his senses and kicked his gambling habit. Then he had to face the consequences of his actions. He had pretended not to know anything about the $2,500 bill on his aunt's credit card. As a result, she believed she had been a victim of credit-card **identity theft**. She reported it as such to her credit-card company.

Then John told his aunt the truth. "She yelled at me, tore into me pretty badly," John says. "To make it up to her, I became her personal servant. I mowed her lawn, took out her trash every day, and cleaned her house."

His aunt wasn't the only family member to lose trust in him. John says his cousins won't even play Monopoly with him. And the friends he swindled in card games have all soured on him, too. "I really screwed up," John says. "Gambling really scars your reputation for life."

are you an
ADDICT?

If you gamble, answer the questions below. Then score yourself.

1. Do your friends gamble a lot?
2. Do you gamble at school?
3. Is gambling more important to you than school or work?
4. Is gambling your most exciting activity?
5. Do you often daydream about gambling?
6. Do you ever borrow money to gamble?
7. When you win at gambling, do you want to gamble again as soon as possible?
8. When you lose at gambling, do you feel you must bet as soon as possible to win back your losses?
9. Do you gamble with money that you intended to use for other purchases such as lunch, clothes, video games, or online music?
10. Do either of your parents gamble?

- If you answered yes to 1 or 2 questions, gambling may have a negative influence on your life.
- If you answered yes to 3 to 5 questions, you are losing control over your gambling.
- If you answered yes to 6 to 10 questions, you have a serious gambling problem and need help. Talk to an adult you trust, and contact one of the following organizations:

NATIONAL COUNCIL ON PROBLEM GAMBLING
Web site: www.ncp gambling.org
E-mail: ncpg@ ncpgambling.org
Phone: (800) 522-4700

GAMBLERS ANONYMOUS
Web site: www.gamblers anonymous.org
E-mail: isomain@ gamblersanonymous.org
Phone: (213) 386-8789

teen parents

"I WAS STUPID."

Nancy's Story

It didn't take long for the teen rebel in Nancy to emerge. After turning 13, she not only broke her mom's rule against dating, she dated a 19-year-old man. Within months, the couple was sexually active, and they didn't use **birth control**. Why? "Because I was stupid," says Nancy, who lives in White Plains, New York. "I knew I could get pregnant, but at that age the possibility of that happening didn't faze me."

It should have. Nancy became pregnant, and nine months later, her daughter, Selena, was born. Nancy was only 14. Three years have passed, and Selena has grown into an active and adorable child, who frequently makes her mom smile. But Nancy, now a high school senior, admits that life as a teen parent is tough. "Selena's wonderful," she says, "but it's so much work raising her."

Each year, **820,000** women under the age of 20 in the United States get pregnant.

Each year, 820,000 women under the age of 20 in the United States get pregnant. "It's hard growing up, and becoming a parent too soon makes it even harder," says Sarah Brown of the National Campaign to Prevent Teen and Unplanned Pregnancy.

Most teen moms end up as single parents. Nearly 80 percent of fathers of children born to teenagers don't marry the mothers. Nancy isn't married to Selena's father, but at least he's around. He lives nearby and comes over nearly every day after work to take Selena to a playground or out for a snack. Nancy cooks dinner every night, and the three of them usually eat together. Selena's father also provides some financial support. "As far as clothes and stuff like that, he buys them for her on an as-needed basis," Nancy says.

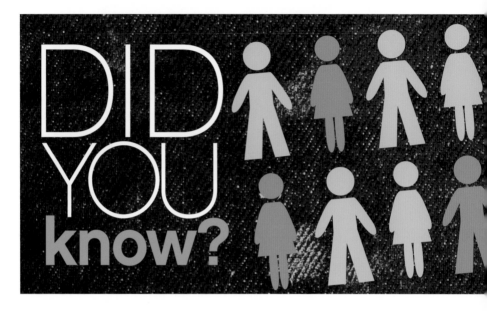

DID YOU know?

Only one-third of teen moms complete high school.

Boys born to teen moms are 13 percent more likely to end up in prison than the sons of older mothers.

Girls born to teen moms are 22 percent more likely to become teen moms themselves than the daughters of older mothers.

About one-quarter of teen mothers have a second child within two years of giving birth to the first one.

Two-thirds of teens younger than 18 who have had sex wish they had waited longer.

But having a child has created tension. "Being young parents is hard," Nancy says. "We've had our ups and downs, but we put up with each other and it seems to work."

Aggie's Story

At least Nancy has some type of a relationship with her child's father. When Aggie of Quincy, Massachusetts, told her boyfriend she was pregnant, he vowed to stay with her. But his enthusiasm for parenthood quickly faded after he learned Aggie was expecting a girl. "He brought me flowers at the ultrasound," Aggie says. "But when he found out I was having a girl, he lost interest. He wanted a son. He tossed the flowers at me and told me he'd meet me outside."

MONEYPIT

Did you know that the cost of raising a child to the age of 18 is between $125,000 and $250,000? (And that's not including college tuition.) In a baby's first year alone, a parent can easily pay between $9,000 and $11,000 for items such as diapers, formula, clothes, and so on. Here are the average yearly prices of some baby items:

CAR SEAT	$35 to $280
CRIB	$160 to $750
STROLLER	$30 to $300
CLOTHES	$500 to $1,200
HIGH CHAIR	$45 to $240
BOTTLES	$10 to $20
FORMULA.	$1,000 to $2,300

And that's just a few items. Among other things a baby needs are a changing table, crib blankets, a playpen, a monitor, a diaper bag, first-aid supplies, a bathtub, and a mobile.

When Aggie gave birth, her boyfriend never showed up at the hospital. He has seen their daughter, Mia, only a handful of times—mostly in court because Aggie has had to force him to pay child support.

Absentee fathers are common. Why don't most teen dads stick around? Most teen boys are emotionally unprepared to be fathers. "They are unsure about their feelings for the baby's mother," says Olivia Campbell, program director for Educating Children for Parenting (ECP), a nonprofit group based in Philadelphia, Pennsylvania. "They're unsure about their feelings about being a dad. And they have been taught that men shouldn't ask for help. They don't know what to do or where to go for help, so many simply go away."

As a result, many teen moms are forced to raise their children alone—while simultaneously living their lives as teenagers. For Aggie, that means waking up at 7 A.M., feeding and dressing Mia, catching the

MANY TEEN **moms are forced to raise their children alone.**

bus at 8:30 A.M., dropping off Mia at day care, and going to school from 9 A.M. to 2:45 P.M. When she can, Aggie does her homework at school.

A Hectic Life

Nancy has a similar schedule, but hers is frequently interrupted. For instance, Selena doesn't like to be separated from her mother, so dropping her off at day care can be difficult. "She starts screaming and throwing a tantrum," Nancy says. "I can't leave until she settles down."

And if Selena is sick, it's Nancy's responsibility to take care of her. This is hard because if Nancy misses too much school, she risks falling behind in her classes. "I'll take care of Selena at night when she's sick, sleep for an hour, and then get dressed and still go to school," Nancy says.

If Selena can't go to day care, and Nancy can't stay

home, the teen has to find someone to watch her child for the day. "It's very stressful when you know that your child is sick and you can't do much about it because you still have to go through with the day," she says.

Even when a baby or small child is healthy, he or she needs constant attention. That means curtailing any social life, often to the point where the only thing teen moms do is watch TV or play with their child. "I watch everyone else have fun," Nancy says. "My friend might be going to a club while I watch *Dora the Explorer* on TV over and over again."

Many teen moms have to work to make ends meet. Three days a week, Aggie works an eight-hour shift as a certified nursing assistant in a nursing home. She punches out at 11 P.M., physically and

"It's very stressful when you know that your child is sick and you can't do much about it."

mentally exhausted. The money she makes goes to Mia's needs. "If I didn't have a child, I would be working to get stuff I want. Now I'm working to get stuff I need: diapers, clothes, baby wipes, shoes. Babies don't stop growing. It's very expensive to have a child."

Having to constantly take care of a child's immediate needs makes it hard for teen moms to improve their own lives. Teen moms are less likely to graduate from high school than their peers. Their limited education, in turn, costs them higher-paying jobs. They are more likely to end up on **public assistance**, or welfare. That's when the government gives money to people who cannot support themselves.

The good news for Nancy and Aggie is that both are determined not to end up on welfare. Nancy's goal, after graduating from high school, is to attend cosmetology school and become a hairdresser. Aggie's goals are even more ambitious. "I want to finish high school, go to college, and become a nurse or work in law enforcement," she says. "I want to set the right example for my daughter. I want to show Mia that you have to do your best to get where you need to go in life."

"I want to set the **RIGHT EXAMPLE** for my daughter."

devoted dad:
Akeem's Story

Not every teenage boy who fathers a child becomes a deadbeat dad. Akeem of Philadelphia, Pennsylvania, and his girlfriend, Ivory, are the parents of seven-month-old Akeem Jr. The teen father never considered abandoning his son, even though friends and teachers told him that he was too young to be a dad. "I had to man-up," Akeem says. "I have a family to take care of."

His stance is admirable because his own father walked out of his life when Akeem was six years old. Despite having no dad role model of his own, Akeem has dedicated himself to fatherhood. He works nights and weekends at a drugstore to provide money for his child, and he and Ivory are still a couple. He has also stayed in school and maintained some balance in his life by doing activities such as playing for his high school football team.

Akeem has also been fortunate enough to be able to ask others for help. Both of the baby's grandmothers baby-sit while Akeem and Ivory are at school. Akeem also takes parenting classes. It's nearly impossible for teens to be successful parents without a support network. "No one gets through this alone," one expert says. "The teen parent needs moms, teachers, doctors, and counselors."

Seeing how the adults in his life have helped him has affected how Akeem views his own role as a dad. "I can't mess around anymore," he says. "I can't hang out on the corner, go to parties, or get in trouble. When I walk out that door, I go to school or work. Then I turn around and come right back."

so long, school

so long, school

"I NEVER FELT LIKE I BELONGED"

Doreen's Story

High school was tough for Doreen. Most of her fellow students ignored her—and when they did notice her, it wasn't for positive reasons. "They teased me about being overweight," she says. "I was shy and didn't talk much. In class, I just waited for the bell to ring."

Doreen wasn't failing classes and admits that she liked math. But the absence of a social life bothered her. "Maybe school is okay if you've got a lot of friends or if you're good at sports. But I never felt like I belonged," she says.

Problems at home made matters worse. "My parents are divorced," Doreen says. "I have a 17-year-old sister who has severe **cerebral palsy**. She can't move on her own and can barely speak. My mom needs help taking care of her and my six-year-old sister. So I spent a lot of time being a baby-sitter for one and a nurse for the other."

Doreen started skipping school more and more. "Eventually, I missed so many days that my teachers and friends assumed I was already gone," she says. "When I told my teachers I was leaving school for good, they never asked me where I was going—or why. Only my job skills instructor tried to talk me out of it, but it was too late."

An estimated **2,500** **students drop out** of school every day in the United States.

An estimated 2,500 students drop out of school every day in the United States.

Doreen was 17 when she dropped out. At first, she was relieved, but then reality set in. "I thought nothing could be worse than school, but I was wrong—really wrong," she says. "I thought I'd be able to go where I wanted, when I wanted. But I didn't have a driver's license. All my friends were in school, so there was no one to hang out with. I took care of my sisters, and I went looking for work."

Doreen tried to get a job as a secretary but was rejected because she didn't have a high school diploma. She ended up working as a maid at a hotel in Jefferson County, Virginia, where she is from. The work is hard, and the pay is low. "I hate this job," she says. "I do the laundry. I spend all day on my feet in a cramped room, folding towels, and dragging wet sheets from the washer to the dryer. All for a lousy $6.25 an hour. But this was the best job I could find without a high school diploma."

Fortunately for Doreen, there is a way out of her dead-end situation. She has earned her **general educational development (GED)** credential, which is equal to a high school diploma and allows her to continue her education. Enrolling in and taking classes to earn her GED wasn't easy, but she did it. And when she passed her GED test, Doreen almost cried tears of relief and joy. "Passing no other test in school ever made me feel as good," she says.

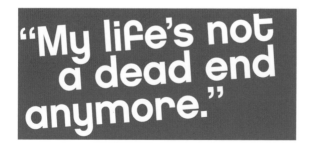

"My life's not a dead end anymore."

BY THE
numbers

"I really accomplished something. I had a graduation ceremony with a maroon cap and gown—stuff I missed when I dropped out. I remember my family letting out a huge cheer when I got my diploma."

Doreen is still working at the hotel, but she has applied to a local community college. "I'm excited about my future," she says. "I want to get a business degree and work in an office. Now when I'm loading the washing machine, I know this job is temporary. My life's not a dead end anymore."

Every day, 2,500 students drop out of school in the United States.

On average, high school dropouts earn $9,200 less per year than people who graduate and more than $1 million less over a lifetime.

Dropouts are four times more likely to be unemployed than teens with a diploma.

Dropouts are three times more likely to be poor than high school graduates.

Dropouts are eight times more likely to be in jail or prison than high school graduates.

Only one in four dropouts returns to school to get a GED.

STOP
and think

Fed up with school? Before you make any impulsive decisions, do the following:

1 Write down what kind of work you hope to do someday. Research the level of education and kinds of classes you need to make that happen. Take charge of your own education.

2 Discuss your situation with an adult you trust and respect.

3 Meet with your guidance counselor to discuss your problems at school.

Taking the Next Step

Graduating from high school is important, but did you know that taking your education even further could really help you succeed in life? Earning a college degree increases your annual income by almost $23,000 a year.

49%
high school
diploma

9%
associate's
degree

27%
bachelor's degree
or higher

DEGREES
of success

In the United States, 85 PERCENT of people over the age of 25 have graduated from high school. Of those, 49 PERCENT did not earn any degrees beyond their diploma, 9 PERCENT went on to earn an associate's degree, and 27 PERCENT achieved a bachelor's degree or higher.

The U.S. Census Bureau reports that adults who have a **bachelor's degree** from college earn $22,909 a year more than adults who only have a high school diploma. Here are the numbers: The average annual income of a college graduate is

$51,554. The average income of a person who graduates from high school and doesn't go on to college is $28,645.

To put those earnings in perspective, calculate how much more a college graduate earns than a person with just a high school diploma over a 40-year span. Why 40 years? That's about the length of time an adult works before retiring. Over a 40-year work career, that extra $22,909 a year adds up to $916,360!

Why is there such a gap between the income of people with college degrees and those without? One reason is the decline of manufacturing jobs in the United States. For instance, the state of New York lost more than 190,000 manufacturing jobs between 2000 and 2005. Traditionally, manufacturing jobs paid quite well and only required a high school diploma. Unfortunately, many of these low-skill jobs have moved to countries where workers can be paid less. In some cases, U.S. manufacturing jobs have been outright eliminated, not moved. In 2006, Ford Motor Company announced the planned closing of 14 plants by 2012, which will eliminate 30,000 jobs.

Kathy Goodman, a guidance counselor at Harding High School in Marion, Ohio, says she strongly encourages all of her students to continue their education after high school. "Most well-paying jobs require some sort of specialized skills that you learn at a university or technical school," she says. "Earning a bachelor's degree or an **associate's degree** is an investment in you and your future."

And it doesn't hurt to remember that it will help your bank account grow a lot, too.

spreading lies

spreading lies

"GETTING OUR FEELINGS OUT..."

Anne's Story

Thirteen-year-old Anne of Austin, Texas, was part of a close group of friends. They hung out all the time and did everything together. But one of the girls, Sophie, began acting unfriendly. "She started saying mean things to us and being annoying," Anne says. "The other two girls and I were upset, so we started talking about her as a way of getting our feelings out and making ourselves feel better."

Talking to others about a problem is normal, but Anne and her friends let things get out of hand. "We started talking about Sophie behind her back all the time," she says. "We talked about her in school, on the phone, and in chat rooms. It got pretty mean."

What Anne and her friends were doing is called **gossiping**. Gossip is the act of spreading rumors and personal information about someone. "Gossip can get out of hand and be really damaging," says Rosalind Wiseman, author of *Queen Bees and Wannabes*, a book about the topic. "The problem occurs when information is exchanged to trash someone's reputation and to put him or her down."

That's the kind of gossip that teenagers experience or engage in frequently. When people gossip in a malicious way, that's an act of

> "We talked about her in school, on the phone, and in chat rooms. It got pretty mean."

aggression—just like bullying a kid in the hallway. Instead of using punches and kicks, gossip uses words and passive behavior—like ignoring a friend—to hurt someone.

Why do teens gossip? In many cases, the gossipers are envious or jealous of someone. "They want to take someone down a notch and put themselves up a notch," says Dr. Elizabeth Berger, a child psychiatrist from Elkins Park, Pennsylvania. "Sometimes they do it because they are hurt, upset, or insecure. And sometimes they just want to be mean."

Spreading rumors also gives gossipers a sense of power. It makes them feel as if they have some control over the people about whom they are gossiping. But in the end, whatever sense of power or rush of adrenaline gossipers get is short-lived. Why?

"Sometimes people gossip because they are **hurt**, **upset**, or **insecure**."

Gossiping is a negative act, and sooner or later, all negative acts crash down on everyone involved.

The first person hurt is the victim. "Some teens are so torn up about it that they don't want to go to school, or they start feeling depressed," Berger says. Sophie, the girl Anne gossiped about, found out from a male student that Anne and the two other friends had called her a bad name. "She freaked out," Anne says. "She told her parents, who contacted the school. Sophie ended up switching

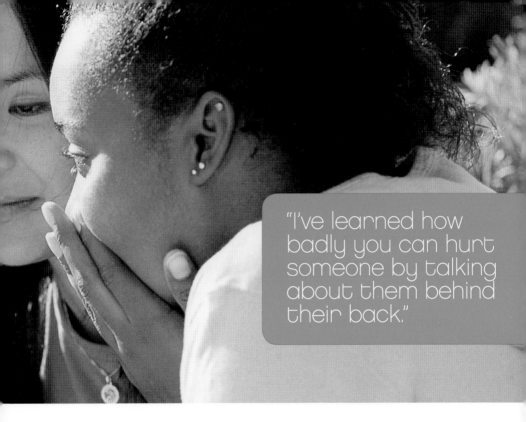

"I've learned how badly you can hurt someone by talking about them behind their back."

schools for a year because of the whole thing. I feel awful about what happened."

The second person or persons victimized are the gossipers. As Anne found out, the guilt gossipers feel when they realize the damage their rumor-spreading causes can be a heavy burden to bear. "I never imagined gossiping could upset someone to the point where they would have to switch schools," Anne says. "I've learned how badly you can hurt someone by talking about them behind their back."

THE GOSSIP WEB

THE INTERNET CAN BE a dangerous place when it comes to spreading gossip. Hiding behind the anonymity of screen names, teens launch vicious attacks against their peers, assuming that they won't be discovered. "Gossip is all about expressing anger and hostility anonymously and indirectly, and the Internet makes that so much easier," Wiseman says.

Rumors started online spread quickly. With a mass e-mail, a blog posting, or a MySpace or Facebook comment, a whole school can hear a story in a matter of minutes. In many cases, the one person who doesn't get the information is the gossip victim.

Jamie, 13, of Rumson, New Jersey, says that girls frequently say negative things about a peer in a chat room, then block the person who's being gossiped about. "Also, people forward and print e-mails, so you have to be really careful about what you write," she says.

YOU BE THE
judge

Read the two scenes to the right. The teens can respond to each situation in different ways. Decide which responses involve gossip and which do not.

SCENE 1:

An upperclassman picks on John in the school parking lot. A third teen, Craig, watches as John backs away and walks quickly into the school.

a. Craig approaches John and tells him that he thinks John should have acted tougher so the guy would stop bullying him. Is this gossip?

b. Craig tells people in the cafeteria what he saw and says that John is a total wimp. Is this gossip?

SCENE 2:

Maria, Kristin, and Jessie are the best of friends and do everything together—until Maria and Jessie get into a huge argument over which one of them they think Kristin likes better.

a. Maria tells Kristin that Jessie said Kristin doesn't look good in any of her clothes. Is this gossip?

b. Afterward, Kristin decides that the fight was stupid and announces to everyone in study hall that Maria and Jessie were fighting over her. Is this gossip?

ANSWERS: In scene 1, response "b" is gossip. In response "a," Craig speaks to John alone to offer his opinion. The conversation is a private one, so it isn't gossip. But in response "b," Craig announces his opinion to a large group of others without John's knowledge or consent. That's gossip.

In scene 2, both responses are gossip. In response "a," Maria talks about Jessie to Kristin behind Jessie's back. In response "b," Kristin talks to others behind both Jessie's and Maria's backs.

painful and permanent

painful and permanent

"I WANT TO FORGET THAT TIME IN MY LIFE"

Fawna's Story

Senior year was a wild time for Fawna. At 17, she was eager to shed her straight-A, good-girl image. She partied hard. She blew off old friends. She even let her grades sink so low that she almost didn't graduate from high school. "I was stupid," Fawna says. "I want to forget that time in my life."

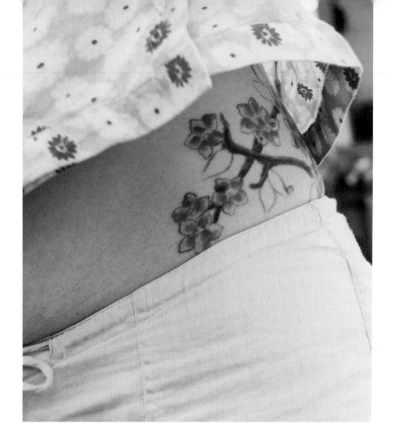

But forgetting hasn't been easy. She has two visual reminders of her not-so-glory days. They are tattoos—a black cat's face on her shoulder and a circle of roses and vines on her stomach. During her senior year, she flaunted her tattoos. Now she regrets getting them. "I definitely wish I hadn't done it," says Fawna, now a college student at the University of California, San Diego. "I am different now. I wish they were gone."

Fawna is getting her wish—sort of. She's having her tattoos removed. Every six weeks, she goes to a **dermatologist**, or skin doctor. Her doctor aims a laser at her shoulder and stomach. Slowly the laser burns off her tattoos. It's a painful procedure. "It feels like a knife slicing off the top layer of your skin," Fawna says. "Sometimes I can even smell it burning."

Fawna never watches the laser cut across her stomach. She closes her eyes and remembers the days when her tattoos seemed new and exciting. At home, she hid them from her parents under sweatshirts. At school, she tossed off the baggy top and strutted down the hallways in a tank top. But for every classmate who told her how great she looked, another would roll his or her eyes at her. "Those students had better heads on their shoulders than I did," Fawna says. "I wish I had paid attention to them."

Here are the truths about tattoos.

- **Teens change, but their tattoos don't.** The interests of most teens and their outlook on life change as they get older. Once out of high school, Fawna changed her mind about her tattoos. She didn't feel like they expressed what she was really about. But her tattoos weren't going anywhere.

- **Tattoos can get infected.** Regulation of tattoo parlors is inconsistent. Myrna Armstrong, a professor of nursing at the Texas Tech University Health Sciences Center, estimates that only 25 percent of tattoo parlors in the United States follow proper safety techniques. For instance, while tattoo parlors in Oregon, Alaska, and Kansas are strictly regulated, in Nevada, only tattoo artists in the city of Reno are expected to follow strict guidelines.

     There are serious health consequences if you are tattooed with equipment that's not sterilized. You could contract a blood-borne disease such as hepatitis or tetanus. You're even at risk of getting HIV, the virus that causes AIDS.

- **Tattoos can be illegal.** Most states prohibit tattooing for people younger than 18, although some allow it with parental consent. Forty-eight states have some laws regarding tattooing and body piercing, but the rules vary from strict to lax.

- ## Removing tattoos is an imperfect—and costly—process.

"Removing a tattoo requires multiple, painful, and expensive treatments," says Dr. Elizabeth Tanzi, co-director of Laser Surgery at the Washington Institute of Dermatologic Laser Surgery. Tanzi removes 600 tattoos a year, but even with her expertise, she says, "there's no guarantee that we can get all of a tattoo off."

Fawna is discovering this. The laser treatments have almost removed the cat's face tattoo on her shoulder, but not the purple rose and green vines on her stomach. Her doctors have warned her that the tattoo may never fully fade.

Most patients must undergo six to 12 tattoo-removal treatments, and some people have to endure up to 30 procedures. It can take more than a year to remove a tattoo, and the process is not cheap. Each of the tattoos cost Fawna $50; removing them will cost more than $2,000. "It's depressing," she says. "When I was in high school, I needed to have these tattoos so badly. I thought I was being so cool. Now I'm paying a huge price."

PIERCING PAIN:
Heidi's Story

Body piercing can be just as dangerous as tattoos. Piercing equipment that is not sterilized can cause blood-borne diseases. Piercings that are not adequately cared for can get infected. And, as with tattoos, most states outlaw piercings for people younger than 18.

Heidi was 14 when she had her belly button pierced. She borrowed her older sister's ID and convinced the piercer in the back room of a clothing shop that she was 18.

But three years later, Heidi thought the jewelry dangling from her navel looked ugly. An avid volleyball player, she had to dive on her side to keep the belly ring from poking her in the stomach. Finally, she removed the jewelry and waited for the piercing to close. It didn't. Instead, Heidi had to see a dermatologist, who surgically removed the scar tissue and sewed up the area. The surgery left an inch-long scar below her belly button.

"I really wish I didn't have that scar," says Heidi, now 19. "Getting pierced was a temporary high and it left me with a permanent scar."

"Getting pierced was a temporary high and it left me with a **PERMANENT SCAR.**"

hero
teen

HE WASN'T LOOKING TO BECOME A HERO

Mack's Story

Mack, 15, had grown up in San Diego, California. He had spent years at the beach and was an experienced ocean swimmer. One day in April 2004, he and his family took a day trip to nearby Newport Beach. He wasn't looking to become a hero, but that's what happened.

While his relatives were lying on the sand, Mack waded out into the water to bodysurf. He noticed two boys playing just a few yards from the shore. They seemed to be about eight or nine years old. As Mack floated nearby, he noticed a troubling sign in the water. On either side of the boys, steady waves lapped the shore. But the boys were standing in oddly calm water.

Mack knew what that meant: **rip current**. A rip current is a powerful flow of water away from the shore. It is caused by waves traveling from deep to shallow water. Sometimes, those waves break in different ways. Some break strongly, others weakly. That makes the water travel in narrow, fast-moving belts. The ground under the current can drop from 3 feet (.91 meters) to more than 20 feet (6.1 m) in one step. And the current can sweep you out to sea in as fast as 8 feet (2.4 m) per second.

Rip currents are deadly. According to the United States Lifesaving Association, 80 percent of beach rescues are due to rip currents—and more than 100 people drown each year when they can't escape the current.

As Mack watched, one of the boy's heads bobbed under the water. Within seconds, the current began dragging him out to sea. Mack yelled at the boy. When the kid didn't answer, Mack swam toward him—right into the current. He grabbed the panicky child's arm and tried to calm him. Mack began to tread water and told the boy to grab his legs. They were going to swim to shore.

80%

Eighty percent of beach rescues are due to rip currents.

Mack knows how to swim in a rip current. "It's useless to fight it and swim headlong into shore," he says. "The current will push you backward." You have to swim sideways until you get out of the current, and then head to shore. But even with this knowledge, the current was too strong. And to make matters worse,

"We were out there for maybe TEN MINUTES but it seemed like **TEN HOURS.**"

the boy was kicking and flailing. Then he jumped onto Mack's shoulders, pushing the teen down in the water.

Swimming was useless; the best thing to do was wait for help. Mack held the boy and assured him everything would be okay. The teen expertly treaded water, allowing the water to slowly move him backward. "We were out there for maybe ten minutes but it seemed like ten hours," Mack says.

Finally, Mack saw a lifeguard's Jeep on the shore. He called out and waved his arms. Within moments, a team of lifeguards with buoys made their way to Mack and the boy. The lifeguards took the boy to shore as Mack swam beside them.

When Mack was sure that the boy was safe, he made his way back to his family. When he reached them, he laid down on a towel, exhausted. "My arms and legs felt like lead," Mack says. Mack didn't tell his family what had happened. "That's just Mack," says his father, who is also named Mack. "He never wants to take credit."

Eventually, lifeguards tracked down the teen to offer their thanks. And later, Mack won an award from the U.S. Lifesaving Association. As one of the lifeguards at the beach told him: "If you hadn't gone out to get that boy, no one would have reached him in time."

Candi's Story

Putting out raging fires, rescuing people trapped in snow, and resuscitating someone who has had a heart attack all sound like responsibilities for the most fearless and experienced firefighter.

But these heroic tasks are all in a day's work for Candi. This 15-year-old teen is part of the Dragon Slayers, a team of six high school students who provide the only round-the-clock emergency medical care to 3,000 people living in a remote area of Alaska. Candi and her fellow Dragon Slayers, who work with the Aniak Fire Department, respond to about 400 calls a year.

Candi decided when she was little that she wanted to become a Dragon Slayer. "I would watch the Dragon Slayers come to my Grandpa's house and check to see what was wrong with him when he was sick," Candi says.

Before she was allowed to become a Dragon Slayer, Candi had to log 240 hours of training in emergency medical services. For months she practiced rappelling cliffs and climbing ladders. Candi also had to learn how to care for burn victims, revive heart-attack patients, and practice the Heimlich maneuver.

Even now that she's a seasoned Dragon Slayer, Candi has to practice hands-on medical skills and rescue drills for at least two hours a week. She also must pass all her classes in school and refrain from drinking alcohol or taking drugs.

Since becoming a Dragon Slayer, Candi and her fellow team members have helped save numerous people who were severely injured or gravely ill. Not every call is life-or-death, but many are. The job is often intense, but the Dragon Slayers have proven year after year that they are up to the task. Indeed, the people of Aniak and the surrounding villages have a lot to be thankful for. Before the Dragon Slayer program started 12 years ago, no emergency medical care existed in the Aniak area.

Candi says that being a Dragon Slayer has helped her figure out a possible career path. "I am thinking about becoming a nurse, and the Dragon Slayer program has helped me prepare for that."

saying no— and meaning it

saying no and meaning it

SHE KNOWS THE CONSEQUENCES

Caitlin's Story

Caitlin, a high school freshman from Peoria, Arizona, saw a cross on the side of the road where five high school kids had died in a drunk driving accident. Right then, she became determined not to drink alcohol or take drugs. Her reason is basic: She knows the consequences and wants to avoid them.

"I always hear stupid stories about things people do when they are high or out-of-control drunk," Caitlin says. "I once heard on the news about a girl who walked into the street and got hit by a car when she was high. . . . Why would I want to do something to hurt myself or someone else?"

She believes that teens abuse substances to escape from the pressures they face—such as fitting in at school, getting good grades, finding time to play on sports teams, and going to parties. "Girls also get stressed out about looking good and wearing the right clothes," she says. "Getting a pimple can ruin a whole week."

Caitlin admits that she gets stressed out, but she copes in positive and healthy ways. She's passionate about her hobbies, which include playing the flute and guitar. She is also a photographer. Her social circle is a source of strength, too. "I relax and enjoy myself by hanging out at the mall and having sleepover parties with my friends," Caitlin says. "We all help each other and listen to each other."

"We all help each other and listen to each other."

Another source of strength is her parents. Her
father is a police officer and has told her stories
about criminals he's arrested who have been high.
Her mother is a preschool teacher who has taught
children with disabilities that were caused by their
parents' drug use.

"What better proof do I need that drugs ruin lives?"

Colleen's Story

A family member was also the inspiration for Colleen to stay away from drugs and alcohol. Colleen is a high school senior in Sellersville, Pennsylvania. Her dad, who had been struggling with drug addiction since his teen years, **overdosed** and died when she was 12. "He had so much to live for but he couldn't see that fact because he was addicted to drugs," she says.

Colleen's dad had been a talented football player in high school, but he injured his knee and was so upset about getting hurt that he turned to drugs to cope. "He took a bad situation and made it worse," Colleen says. "What better proof do I need that drugs ruin lives?"

SUBSTANCE ABUSE AT HOME

13% of kids under 18 years of age live in a household where a parent or other adult uses illegal drugs.

24% of kids live in a household where a parent or other adult is a binge drinker or heavy drinker.

drugs
at school

Many teens see drugs every day on the grounds of their schools. For these kids, it can be even harder to say no. Compared to teens at drug-free schools, they are:

16 times likelier to use an illegal drug other than marijuana or prescription drugs;

15 times likelier to abuse prescription drugs;

6 times likelier to get drunk at least once a month;

5 times likelier to use marijuana;

4 times likelier to smoke cigarettes.

If you go to a school where drugs are around, Web sites such as www.abovetheinfluence.com and www.checkyourself.com can help you get the information you need to make smart choices about substance abuse.

Colleen is an athlete herself and uses basketball as a positive outlet for any stress she feels. Like Caitlin, Colleen also uses her social circle to stay out of trouble. "We watch movies, go bowling, or go out for dinner and just laugh," she says. "As long as we're hanging out with friends, we have a great time."

Both teens realize that the pressure to succumb to substance abuse will always be present. But both have a strong resolve not to give in to that pressure. "I am confident that I can stick to my beliefs," Caitlin says. "Every time I choose not to drink or do drugs, my self-esteem gets stronger. I feel better about myself."

Colleen openly says she's proud of the fact that she's never drunk alcohol or tried drugs. "How many high school students can say that?" she says. "I consider it a real accomplishment. It's part of my identity now. I am someone who is drug-free."

DECISION Time

1 You're leaving a party when you realize the person who's giving you a ride has been drinking. When you ask her about it, she says, "I feel totally sober, don't worry!" What should you do?

a. Make a face, think about how short the drive is, and get in the car.

b. Insist on sitting in the front seat so that you can grab the wheel if she does anything reckless or dangerous.

c. Tell her you make it a rule not to ride with anyone who's had even one drink. Call a friend or family member and ask that person to come and pick you both up.

2 You find out that your date for the school dance has sneaked a thermos of alcohol into the event. What should you say?

a. "Wow, you are the best date ever! Let's go get wasted."

b. "That makes me nervous. So I'll just have one small drink."

c. "We could get into a lot of trouble if we get caught with that. And, we don't need to drink to have fun. Let's dance."

RECOMMENDED: (1) c; (2) c. But you already knew that, right?

5 ways to stay SUBSTANCE free

Before you go to a party, make up your mind not to drink or take drugs. The earlier you decide not to drink, the more comfortable you'll be with your decision.

Be up-front when declining drugs or alcohol. Say that you're not doing either and drop the issue. "If you don't make a big deal out of not drinking, then the people drinking will realize that it's not a big deal," says Brendan, who hasn't had a drink in five years and is a youth director for Mothers Against Drunk Driving (MADD).

Attend parties with friends who don't drink or take drugs. "It's hard to face peer pressure by yourself," says one girl named Jakenna. "It helps to be with people who agree with you."

Hold a cup with soda in it. Often, nondrinkers are targeted because they're not holding anything. But if it looks like you have alcohol in a cup, drinkers are less likely to hassle you. "The only times I've been questioned is if I'm standing there *without* a cup in my hands," Brendan says.

Leave the scene. If you don't feel comfortable at a party, leave. Drive home or get a ride.

stepping up

stepping up

"WE NEED TO DO SOMETHING"

Amelia's Story

Amelia was riding in a car on her way to her aunt's house for Thanksgiving dinner when she saw a group of homeless people standing in line outside a soup kitchen. "We were going to have this big meal with our family, and those people had to go to a soup kitchen to eat," she says. "I noticed that none of them were wearing socks. I told my mom, 'We need to do something to help these people.'"

The image of seeing people barefoot or in shoes without socks stuck with her. "When my feet get cold, my whole body gets cold, so I figured that's what happened to them," Amelia says. "They don't have anywhere to go to get warm, so I thought socks would make a difference."

They have. Amelia was nine years old when she got inspired to help the homeless. Six years later, the Livermore, California, teen has distributed more than 60,000 pairs of socks to those in need. Her success is due to her own determination, her boldness when it came to asking both big and small organizations for help, and her willingness to work hard to achieve her goals.

Amelia didn't waste time getting started. Right after the Thanksgiving break, she began asking for **donations** of socks from members of her church, classmates, and Girl Scout troops. Her efforts resulted in some much-needed publicity when a local newspaper wrote an article about her program. Amelia took the article to area stores and asked for their help. To her delight, they signed on, and her program took off.

For the first few years, Wal-Mart provided her with 700 pairs of socks every couple of months. The Oakland Raiders of the National Football League contributed extra-large socks. And donations poured in from area students and businesses. Amelia even struck gold at a local convention of real estate agents. After delivering a speech about her program at the convention, several companies in attendance decided to support her cause. In all, Amelia received $3,000 in donations. She used the generous gifts to expand her program. Now, in addition to collecting socks, she also supplies homeless shelters with towels and diapers.

Her program has grown tremendously, but Amelia still keeps her operation a family affair. With the help of her mom and sister, she regularly delivers socks to 17 shelters in the San Francisco area. When weather conditions are poor, the trio often hands out socks to individuals who are living on the streets. "The first time I did that, I wasn't sure how the people were going to react, so I was nervous," Amelia says. "Now I know they're responsive, so I'm not. They're always thankful."

Here's one example. Amelia approached a middle-aged woman who was living underneath a highway overpass. "She was huddled with all her stuff," Amelia says. "It was really cold. She had duct tape around her feet. It looked really tight. She said it hurt. She took a few pairs of socks and thanked us. She said, 'God bless you.'"

Although Amelia has received multiple honors and awards for her volunteer efforts, she explains that the most gratifying part of her work is visiting the homeless people she serves. "When I go to the street, I get to see who is actually getting to use the socks," she says. "It lets me know that I am actually making a difference in people's lives. That's important to me."

VOLUNTEERING

- Helps people in need
- Builds your self-esteem
- Gives you experience working
- Helps beat feelings of boredom
- Helps overcome a loss you have experienced
- Helps gain perspective on life. There's no better way to recognize the good things in your life than to help people in need.

before YOU COMMIT

Volunteering to help others is a great thing to do, but doing so takes a mature commitment. Before you sign up, make sure you . . .

HAVE THE TIME. Teens are really busy. They have school, extracurricular activities, active social lives, family obligations, and maybe even part-time jobs. Only volunteer if you know that you can commit to the people you're helping.

CARE ABOUT THE CAUSE. Don't volunteer for a cause unless you fully believe in it. And it's important to enjoy doing the work you'll be doing. For example, if you're not a cat or dog person, it's a bad idea to volunteer to work at an animal shelter!

10

GREAT

GREAT
places to
volunteer

FOOD BANKS: Workers at food banks collect food, manage the inventory, and distribute food to those in need. Food banks are especially active during the holidays.

SPECIAL OLYMPICS: The Special Olympics provides year-round sports training and athletic competition for children and adults with mental disabilities. Volunteer activities include sports training, fund-raising, competition planning, and administrative help.

HABITAT FOR HUMANITY: This organization builds and gives houses to people in need. Volunteers not only help others but can learn a great deal about construction work.

STATE PARKS: Volunteers can learn about conservation, park maintenance, and trail construction.

LIBRARIES: Many libraries need help reshelving books, running children's programs, and making books available to the community.

SENIOR CITIZEN CENTERS: Volunteers spend time doing activities or just hanging out with elderly people who need friendly companionship.

ANIMAL SHELTERS: Many animal shelters are nonprofit organizations and welcome volunteers to help take care of animals and keep facilities clean.

RED CROSS: Volunteers for the American Red Cross help people after disasters like earthquakes and floods. They may also assist in efforts to help individuals, such as a small child who is sick and needs blood.

SALVATION ARMY: This organization provides social services, rehabilitation centers, disaster services, and character-building activities for people of all ages.

POLITICAL CAMPAIGNS: During election years, there are many opportunities to get involved in national and local political campaigns. Pick a candidate whose ideas you support.

CA$H
for care

Raising money for charity is a great way to help people in need. There are many ways to have a fund-raiser. Car washes, bake sales, and auctions are all great ideas. The following tips can help you meet your goal.

PICK

Pick a cause you care about. It will be easier to stay committed if you believe in the charity.

RESEARCH

"Make sure you are supporting a legitimate charity and not a scam," says Sandra Miniutti of Charity Navigator, an organization that evaluates charities. Also, make sure the charity uses its money efficiently. "A charity should be using at least 75 percent of its money on programs," she says.

SPREAD THE WORD

The more people who know about your fund-raiser, the more money you can take in. If you're having a school bake sale, hang up fliers and make announcements. If you're doing a community-wide event such as a car wash, contact your local newspaper or radio station to get the word out to a lot of people.

REWARDS

Fund-raisers need volunteers to be successful. To encourage people to participate, provide free cookies to volunteers. Line up discounts on sports events or movie tickets. You can offer them as prizes to your volunteers once they reach fund-raising targets.

GOALS

Determine how much money you want to raise before you begin. Having a specific amount will help you plan how to make your goal a reality.

APPRECIATION

You can never say "thank you" enough—to both your volunteers and your donors. Throwing a party after the fund-raiser is a great way to show you care, while injecting some fun into a worthy cause.

associate's degree—a degree granted after a two-year course of study, especially by a community or junior college

bachelor's degree—a degree granted by a college or university after a four-year course of study

birth control—the practice of using contraception (condoms, birth control pills, etc.) to prevent unwanted pregnancy

cerebral palsy—a condition marked by impaired muscle coordination and oftentimes speech and learning disabilities, typically caused by damage to the brain before or at birth

dermatologist—a doctor who specializes in the treatment of skin diseases

donations—goods, services, or a sum of money given to a charitable cause

general educational development (GED)—a credential awarded to those who successfully complete a required test in place of a typical four-year high school program

gossiping—the spreading of rumors that focus primarily on the personal or private lives of other people

identity theft—the stealing of another person's official or financial information (such as a credit card number or Social Security number), usually with the purpose of making purchases or financial gain

incarcerated—to be imprisoned

juvenile detention facility—a state-run facility that aims
to make minors with criminal records ready for reintegration
into society by providing them with therapy and a healthy,
regimented schedule

larceny—the theft of another person's property

limbic system—a complex system of nerves and networks
in the brain, involving several areas that affect a person's
instincts and moods; it controls the basic emotions (fear,
pleasure, anger, etc.) and drives (hunger, sex, dominance,
care of offspring)

magnetic resonance imaging (MRI)—a form of imaging
that hospitals use to evaluate a person's body tissue and
internal organs

overdosed—to have dangerously and excessively
overconsumed a drug

prefrontal cortex—the foremost part of the prefrontal lobe of
the brain that functions primarily during decision making and
impulse control

public assistance—government benefits provided to the
needy, usually in the form of cash or vouchers

rip current—a strong surface current flowing out to sea from the
shore

Books

Barna, George. *Real Teens: A Contemporary Snapshot of Youth Culture*. Ventura, CA: Regal Books, 2001.

Cherniss, Hilary, and Sara Jane Sluke. *The Complete Idiot's Guide to Surviving Peer Pressure for Teens*. Indianapolis: Alpha, 2001.

Desetta, Al, and Sybil Wolin, eds. *The Struggle to Be Strong: True Stories by Teens About Overcoming Tough Times*. Minneapolis: Free Spirit Publishing, 2000.

Englander, Anrenee. *Dear Diary, I'm Pregnant: Teenagers Talk About Their Pregnancy*. Toronto: Annick Press, 1997.

Esherick, Joan. *Dying for Acceptance: A Teen's Guide to Drug- and Alcohol-Related Health Issues*. Broomall, PA: Mason Crest, 2004.

Haddock, Patricia. *Teens and Gambling: Who Wins?* Berkeley Heights, NJ: Enslow Publishers, 1996.

Jacobs, Thomas. *They Broke the Law—You Be the Judge: True Cases of Teen Crime*. Minneapolis: Free Spirit Publishing, 2003.

Weill, Sabrina Solin. *We're Not Monsters: Teens Speak Out About Teens in Trouble*. New York: HarperTempest, 2002.

Online Sites & Organizations

The National Campaign to Prevent Teen and Unplanned Pregnancy

teenpregnancy.org
1776 Massachusetts Ave. NW
Suite 200
Washington, DC 20036
(202) 478-8500
This site provides a very extensive array of data, facts, and news reports on the problem of teen pregnancy in the United States.

Partnership for a Drug-Free America

checkyourself.com
Partnership for a
Drug-Free America
405 Lexington Avenue
Suite 1601
New York, NY 10174
This hip Web site provides teens with stories, quizzes, blogs, facts, and videos about the problems that result from drug and alcohol abuse.

KidsPeace

teencentral.net
1-800-8KID-123
This site provides teens with a broad list of help lines in every state and also allows them to post their own personal stories and read the stories of others.

Juvenile Delinquency

safeyouth.org/scripts/topics/delinquency.asp
National Youth Violence
Prevention Resource Center
P.O. BOX 10809
Rockville, MD 20849-0809
This site provides national stats, psychological studies, personal stories, and external links to other organizations that address the problem of juvenile delinquency. The Web site also provides "safeyouth" specialists who are ready to discuss problems of teen crime.

Author's Note

Bob Hugel is the editor of *Scholastic Choices* magazine, a family and consumer science, health, and life skills publication read by students in middle school and high school. Teachers subscribe to *Choices* and use the magazine with their respective curricula. The goal of *Choices*, which has been in publication for more than 20 years, is to help teenagers make responsible decisions regarding their present and future lives. Teachers or administrators looking for information about *Choices* magazine can call Scholastic's customer service department at 1-800-724-6527 or go to www.scholastic.com/choices.

Bob would like to thank the writers who wrote the original articles on which the content of *I Did It Without Thinking* is based. Each author provided quality research, accurate reporting, and lively writing in their articles.

Bob lives in Maplewood, New Jersey, with his wife and two children.